We Were Innocent

A Childhood on a Post-Civil War Plantation

Evelyn Fuqua Ph.D.

Bandon, Oregon

2019

We Were Innocent

A Childhood on a Post-Civil War Plantation

For information address:
P.O. Box 341
Bandon, Oregon 97411

www.evelynfuqua.com

ISBN: 978-0-9850091-5-1
Published by O.M.R.A.
Bandon, Oregon 97411

"Evolution is the emergence of that which already is in form, in an ever-upward spiraling. The whole process of evolution is to produce a being that can consciously cooperate with the Evolutionary Principle, which is Pure Spirit."

Ernest Holmes

Dedication

To my beloved nurse Laura, Old Carrie, Old Hiram and all the other brave Colored people who lived on our farm.

Acknowledgements

My great appreciation and gratitude to:

My brother, Ralph Bassett, who gave me input on our family history on numerous occasions

My cousin, Patsy Hilliard, who refreshed my memory of our many childhood activities

My niece Kitsie Riggall and her husband Chris who encouraged me to write what I could remember about the Bassett history.

My beloved husband, Paul, who gave me constant support and computer assistance in formatting this book and solving all the other computer questions that arose during the birthing of this manuscript. Paul also graciously allowed me to include his story about his early history of working in the Kentucky tobacco fields during the depression years. He used his considerable writing skills to give me valuable input and editing suggestions.

The ladies of the Fort Valley Chapter of the Daughters of the American Revolution (DAR) for their work in compiling *History of Peach County Georgia*, a valuable reference for wills describing ownership of slaves.

Sue Bassett Folawn for her book *Homeplace,* a history and genealogy of the Bassett family.

Morris Dees, author of *A Lawyer's Journey,* and founder of the Southern Poverty Law Center which continues to fight for civil rights in this country.

Michael Phelan who formatted this book for publication in paperback form and Kindle; he also used his considerable artistic talent for designing an appropriate cover.

About the Author

Evelyn Fuqua Cook Ph.D. was born in Fort Valley, Georgia in 1932. She eventually migrated to California where she had a successful 33 year career as a teacher and counselor in the public schools. After retiring from the school system, Dr. Fuqua went into private practice, specializing in past life regression therapy. A client who was an extraterrestrial Walk-In led her to explore the ET phenomena. Using her metaphysical background, she has previously written four books. *We Are Innocent* is quite different from her earlier books, but she feels it is an important book to write during this present time in our history.

Dr. Fuqua holds a B.A. in psychology from Agnes Scott College in Decatur, Georgia; a M.A. in Counseling from Sacramento State University and Ph.D. in Psychology from the Professional School of Psychology.

She and her husband, Paul, are enjoying life in beautiful Bandon on the Southern Oregon coast.

Table of Contents

Preface

Some of the terminology used in this book is taken directly from the wills of individuals who owned slaves. It is quite offensive to most people in this day and age. I am also using the terminology for African Americans even after the Civil War. I apologize if any of this is offensive to my readers, but my intent is to accurately describe the way these brave people were regarded during the time I was growing up. We need to remember that our country has come a long way since then but still has quite a ways to go to give equality for all.

Introduction

As the readers of my earlier books know, I have previously written about metaphysical/spiritual material gleaned from my many years in private practice as a therapist. However, as I have grown older and listened to all the news about Black Lives Matter, The MeToo movement and various other contemporary issues, I have reflected a great deal on my childhood, growing up three miles from Fort Valley, Georgia on a large farm with numerous Colored people living in houses on our farm. How has this affected my life and thinking?

While I was not born until 1932, the house where I was born is located on land that formerly was a slave plantation. The Blacks who lived on our place were referred to as the "Hands". However, as a child I thought of them as the Colored. I heard the term Negroes, but it was seldom used. I did hear some people call them the "N" word, although no one in my immediate family did this. Growing up I just accepted the extreme poverty and poor living conditions of the Colored people as just the way it was. Since "Colored" people was the terminology mainly used when I was growing up, that is the term I will use in this book although my brother Ralph, who inherited the farm when my father died, tells me that he and Boble (my father) always referred to the Colored as "the hands". My hope is that writing this will contribute my little bit to everyone's understanding of how brave these people were and life in the country before any of our modern conveniences. They are part of my history and the history of my family. The Colored people on our farm were like my extended family. They were true survivors of a very difficult life.

Addressing the situation of the Colored on our place was my original intention for writing this book, but recently my niece and her husband who live in Atlanta, Georgia, flew out to visit me and my husband, Paul at our home in Bandon, Oregon. They both have extremely busy work schedules so we were honored that they took the time and considerable expense to visit us. One of our in-depth conversations was regarding life in general for a child growing up on a former slave plantation. They encouraged me to document all of the events I remember from my early life since I am at the advanced age of 87 and I am one of only four remaining Bassetts from our branch of the family, all of us quite elderly. While very personal, it is also an interesting bit of history. I have so many questions I wish I had asked my parents when they were alive, but I imagine that is true of a great many people. The facts I give are true as far as I know, but my memory is a bit foggy on some events so my stories may not be 100 % accurate.

Please join me on a visit to a time that truly is "gone with the wind".

Chapter 1

Early History of Fort Valley, Georgia

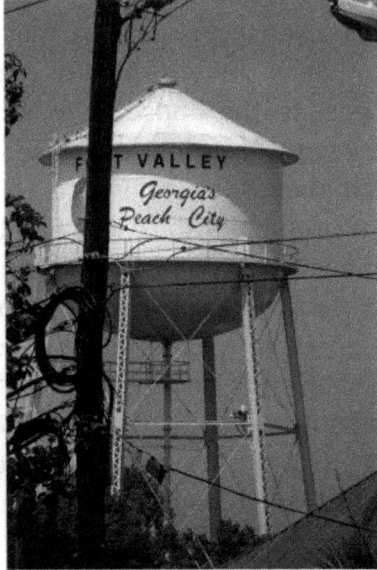

Fort Valley water tower.

Prior to 1821 the area encompassed by Peach and its nearby counties had been a part of the vast hunting grounds of the Creek Indian Nation. This territory was obtained by a treaty with the Indians at Indian Springs in 1825. The history of early Georgia is largely the history of the Creek Indians since during most of the colonial period, Creeks outnumbered both European colonists and enslaved Africans and occupied more of the land than these newcomers. However, the Creek nation was a relatively young political entity. When Christopher Columbus arrived in the Americas, no such nation existed. At that time most Southeastern natives lived in centralized

1

mound-building societies whose achievements are still visible today as the Etowah mounds at Cartersville and the Ocmulgee National Monument in Macon. The Spanish incursions into the southeast in the sixteenth century devastated these people. European diseases such as smallpox may have killed 90 percent or more of the native population, but by the end of the 1600's Southeastern Indians began to recover. They built a complex political alliance, which united native peoples from the Ocmulgee River west to the Coosa River, but traders began applying it to every native resident of the Tallapoosa Rivers in Alabama. Although they spoke a variety of languages, the Indians were united in their wish to remain at peace with one another. By 1715 English newcomers from South Carolina were calling these allied peoples "Creeks". The term was shorthand for Indians living on Ochese Creek near Macon, but traders began applying it to every native resident of the Deep South. They numbered about 10,000 at that time. Early interaction between Creeks and colonists centered on the exchange of slaves and deerskins for foreign products like textiles and kettles. Soon after the establishment of South Carolina in 1670 the Creeks had set up a brisk business capturing and selling Florida Indians to their new neighbors. By 1750 this kind of trade had nearly disappeared for lack of demand (by then slave trade from Africa had started). Many Georgia newcomers were African slaves, and they forged ties with the Creek Indians. Over the course of the eighteenth century, hundreds of fugitive slaves settled in Creek towns. This encouraged the Creek people to oppose slavery. The new state of Georgia viewed the Indians as an impediment to the expansion of plantation slavery rather than as partners in trade. Under pressure by Georgia, Creeks ceded their lands east of the Ocmulgee River in three separate treaties. At the same time, the United States initiated a program to turn Creeks into ranchers and planters.

Although some Creeks willingly embraced the program, many opposed it.

Tension between the two factions was so enormous that it erupted in civil war in 1813. Finally in 1814 the Creeks were soon dispossessed of their remaining land. The following year Creek representatives signed the Treaty of Washington, ceding their remaining Georgia land.

Georgia citizens played a central role in removing the 20,000 Creeks still in the Southeast. Andrew Jackson led a force that killed 800 Creeks in battle. The Red Stick War, as it was called, officially ended in August 1814 with the Treaty of Fort Jackson. In this agreement the Creeks were forced to cede 22 million acres, including a huge tract in southern Alabama. In 1832 the Creeks signed a treaty agreeing to their relocation to Indian Territory (later known as Oklahoma). Land speculators based in Columbus, Georgia, saw opportunity in the Creeks' misfortune. They illegally purchased Creek lands and then secretly encouraged hostilities between whites and Indians, hoping to spark a war that would clear the Southeast once and for all of its native residents. They found success in a brief conflict between the United States and Creeks in 1836. At its conclusion, U.S. troops, assisted by Georgia and Alabama militia and General Winfield Scott, forcibly rounded up Creeks and sent them to Indian Territory west of the Mississippi under the watchful eye of armed soldiers, many of the Indians in chains.

None of this was ever taught in Georgia schools. I was aware that the Cherokee Indians were sent to Oklahoma, many of them dying on their long journey by foot. This, the so-called Veil of Tears, was mainly further north in the Carolinas where the Cherokees were driven out, but we in Georgia, were not aware of our similar mistreatment of the Indians.

Many of the first settlers in Fort Valley were from the older counties of Georgia, descendants of those Virginians and Carolinians who a century earlier had been attracted to the state. Other settlers in 1832 were well-to-do planters from the Orangeburg district of South Carolina who wished to concentrate upon the cultivation of cotton.

A post office was established at Fort Valley, on December 7, 1825. It was chartered as a town on March 3, 1856 with commissioners empowered to make laws and regulations for a government in the best interest of the citizens. It is noted that a precedent was shattered in 1962 when a female mayor assumed office after seventy-four years of white male dominance. Many years later there were several Colored mayors, elected mainly by the majority population which has always been Colored.

Most of the white families in the early days had slaves. According to *The History of Fort Valley* published in 1972 by the Daughters of the American Revolution, one of the servants stood and waved a fly-brush of peafowl feathers over the table at each meal. The master had his valet; and the mistress, her maid. It would have been considered disgraceful for the mistress to do any housework, such as cleaning, sweeping, dusting, or cooking, but she did know how to have the work properly done. This was still true to a large extent when I was growing up. My mother always had a cook and someone to clean. This was true of all of my family's friends. About the only time Mama ever fixed a meal was Sunday night when the cook was off. This was usually tuna fish sandwiches.

I, consequently, never learned to cook. When I graduated from college, my father gave me a case of tuna fish, knowing that my roommate and I would probably do very little cooking. Our only attempt at a "real" meal was a whole chicken which was frozen and refused to cook. I think we finally gave up and threw it out! Of course, when I married at 23, I did manage to cook after a fashion by reading a cook book.

Most of the information on ownership of slaves is from probate of wills. James A. Everett, one of the earliest residents of Fort Valley stated in his will written in 1848: "To my beloved wife, Mary Beaufort, I give the sum of fifteen thousand dollars, which amount my executors are required to lay out in the purchase of Negroes for her, subject to the following conditions: the Negroes purchased not to be liable to sale or subject to debts contracted by herself or any future husband. If she should contract any marriage hereafter and have children by such marriage, the property purchased in accordance with this clause to be the property of herself and the children of such marriage if the children survive her. In the event of her death without any future marriage then the said Negroes are to revert to my estate." Apparently all of this was well thought out, but there is no mention of freeing the slaves. He states further in his will that he bequeathed to the daughters of his deceased sister the sum of one thousand dollars each and this is to be used for purchasing Negroes for the legatees. Everett gave his nephew two thousand dollars which was required to purchase Negroes for him. To his sister-in-law he gave four thousand dollars to be used by his executors to purchase slaves for her. To his brothers-in-law he bequeathed four thousand dollars each, to be invested by his executors for them in slaves. Finally to his mother-in-law he gave the use for life of the following Negroes: Early, Caroline, Burrlee, Tatnell and Jerry. After her death, said Negroes were to revert to his estate.

Obviously slaves represented wealth. Maybe to soothe his conscience, he gave five hundred dollars to purchase a Negro man or boy for Rev. John Fulwood. Further his will states that all remaining Negro property (slaves) shall go to his daughter and her husband.

In another couple's marriage settlement (I presume like a dowry) they were given certain Negroes: King, a man about 39 years of age, Dick, a man about 26, Tom, about 21 , Frank, a boy about 12, Priscilla, a woman about 28 as well as Priscilla's three children, Martha, about 7, Ella about 5 and Simon about 18 months old, Louisa, a woman about 24 and her 2 year old daughter, Caroline, about 34, Simon, about 58 and Rachel about 62. Since no birth records were kept, the age of slaves and date of birth were always approximate.

In my own family the first mention of slaves was in 1810. William Bassett left two slaves each to his sons, Stephen and Thomas and two to his daughter Francis. In the will he bequeathed to his wife one Negro named Jim; to Stephen Bassett one Negro fellow called Will and one Negro girl named Ester. "Thirdly I do give to Francis Bassett one Negro wench (girl?) named Frank, and one Negro girl named Hannah. Fourthly, I bequeath unto Thomas Bassett one Negro wench called Harriet and one Negro child called Fanny." Although I can find no actual records of ownership of slaves after the above, there no doubt were slaves up until the emancipation which brings me to the next chapter about the Bassett plantation.

Chapter 2

Bassett Early History

My Great Grandfather's tombstone.

Francis Bassett purchased 378 acres in South Carolina in April 1786 in the eleventh year of the Independence of the United States. He served as a sergeant with the South Carolina State Militia, having emigrated from England before the Revolutionary War. There was a period of heavy migration from the Carolinas to Georgia as settlers tried for land offerings in Georgia land lotteries. Only people who had been residents of Georgia for three or more years were eligible for the lottery. One of the sons, Stephen Bassett, first settled near Ft. Hawkins close to Macon, Georgia when that part of the state was still on the frontier and the Indians still inhabited that area. In 1828

7

Stephen purchased 202 acres in Houston County for $250. The property was approximately a mile and a half southeast of Byron, Georgia. This area subsequently was part of a new county named Peach County due to the large number of peach orchards and packing plants later located around Fort Valley. This is where the Bassetts settled permanently. The land was rich but forested and needed to be cleared in order to plant crops. Roads were few and primitive. In time the family would purchase additional land for a total of 1000 acres by the time I was born.

Bassett Cemetery plot.

The Civil War brought great tragedy to the family with the loss of three grandsons in the service. Two grandchildren also died of illness during this time (1863). Stephen left his property to his wife Jane who left it to her sons William and Stephen. The Civil War ended May 9, 1865 and the emancipation of slaves was January 1, 1863. Stephen Hicks Basset purchased the Bassett homeplace from his father, Stephen Elisha. Since the original purchase of the Bassett land was in 1828, there were slaves on the plantation at that time. After slaves were emancipated, many of them stayed on at the plantations where they had been owned. This was probably a necessity since most could not read and had no real way of earning a living away from the plantation. This apparently was the case on the Bassett farm because there was an area with four houses we all called "the quarters", an obvious reference to slave quarters.

I was born in 1932 in the old family home. As was usual in those days, mine was a home birth. The house was a rambling "shotgun" type with a central hallway with two rooms on each side. Three were used as bedrooms and the fourth was the "parlor". The central hallway was large enough to have sofas and chairs, therefore, was often used as a living area since the parlor was reserved for company and special occasions, like Christmas. There were wraparound porches, one leading to what was probably an addition with two rooms which were the living quarters of my father and mother until nine years after my birth when my father was able to build a large home across the road (much later a paved road). Between this addition and the rest of the house was a passageway connected to a kitchen. The dining room was between the kitchen and one of the bedrooms. All of the porches were screened except the long front porch. This was necessary to keep out the many insects and to help somewhat with the hot, humid summers. The only heat source was a fireplace in every room and a big wood stove in the kitchen. We used kerosene lamps at night since there was no electricity. I remember sitting on my father's lap as he read me stories by lamp light.

My father and his brother had inherited the house and farm together so my Uncle Ralph's family lived in the main part of the house since he had five daughters, and my father, mother, little brother and I lived in the addition. Three bathrooms had been added to the house prior to my birth, but there was still an outhouse out back located in what was then a large chicken yard. Patsy, my cousin, and I often used the outhouse when we were out playing. I remember using Sears Roebuck catalogues for toilet paper.

Mama, Grandmama, Grandpapa, brother Ralph and Boble.

My Aunt Henriette always seemingly hated my mother and seldom allowed her in the kitchen although both families ate together in the dining room. There was a very large dining room table which apparently had room to seat four adults and six children. My little brother Ralph probably sat in a high chair when he was small, but he was five by the time we moved to our new house so that would have made eleven people. I'm not sure how that worked but I have clear memories of both families sitting at the dining room table together. There was a cook, but Aunt Henriette made it clear that she was the boss of the house. I surmised that she disliked my mother because my father brought his very pretty new wife to the house to live. My aunt was quite overweight, having given birth to five daughters. Also, my Uncle Ralph was very fond of my mother which didn't help the situation. One of the daughters was named Edith after my mother, but according to my cousin, my aunt insisted that name never be used. Instead she was always Patsy. To this day that is what she is called.

It must have been a difficult life for Mama. She later told me that when she first moved to the farm there were no bathrooms as well as no electricity. She had grown up in Opelika, Alabama; then her family moved to Decatur, Georgia. Since she had never been to the farm before marriage, it must have been a big culture shock being in the country with no city conveniences. Mama's father worked for a large hardware company as a salesman traveling all over the state of Georgia during the week. Grandpapa was almost completely deaf due to a childhood illness; he could not drive so had a Colored chauffeur named Emory. I wonder where Emory slept during all this travel. During that period of Georgia history, he certainly did not sleep in the lodging where Grandpapa stayed. There was never any discussion of this, and no one living now knows the answer. Apparently Emory was well thought of by the family and he was very loyal to my grandfather.

My father's brother, my Uncle Ralph, had been wounded in World War I. When he returned home, he was not able to do anything very physically demanding which meant my father had to take over the farm after their parent's died in order to keep the property in the family. Apparently Uncle Ralph was able to work for Metropolitan Life Insurance Company since he was quite outgoing and I imagine was an excellent salesperson. My uncle served in the Marines at the battle front nearly a year, where he was severely wounded. After being discharged from the hospital, he was assigned to the circulation department of the Provost Marshall in Paris. He was promoted to Captain just before the signing of the Armistice. It was in Paris where he met Aunt Henriette. She was a translator so spoke English quite well before coming to Georgia as a war bride. No doubt she had the same culture shock when she arrived at the farm!

Mama met Boble (I tried to say his name, Noble, as a small child but it came out Boble which stuck until he died) through Uncle Ralph. Met Life had a main office in Atlanta which my uncle would visit quite often on business. Mama worked at Metropolitan Life as a secretary. She had attended Agnes Scott College for three years but dropped out when her two brothers were old enough to go to college and they needed Mama and her twin sister, Aunt Evelyn, to go to work so the boys could go to college. Apparently the education of the boys was more important than the education of the girls. Uncle Roger and Uncle John went on to become Presbyterian ministers; they served as Chaplains in World War II. The whole family remained close, including the younger child, Aunt Kitsie, until they scattered and had families of their own. Mama was 30 years old when she married Boble. From some of her remarks, I gathered that she was very taken with several young men during her youth but for unknown reasons things didn't work out. I always thought she loved Boble but life on the farm was difficult for her; however, the Bassetts were considered one of the "best" families in Fort Valley and she very much enjoyed her title as "Mrs. Noble P. Bassett". It definitely gave her status in our small town! Mama was a charming Libra and I am an Aquarian. I was a "good" daughter doing all the socially acceptable things such as attending all kinds of very boring parties. It was also very important to be dressed properly. I was never in any trouble, but I recall a lot of rebellious talk during my teen years. I adored my father who was also an Aquarian, and I had the impression that Mama was rather jealous of my relationship with my father. I probably was quite spoiled since Boble was 40 when I was born and I was his first child. He and I always seemed to be on the same mental wave length. He died of cancer when I was only 28. My husband had taken a job in California in 1959, but when I was told that Boble probably did not have very long to live, I dropped all of the classes I was taking at Sacramento State College to fly back and be with him during his last three weeks. I am not one to cry very much, but the tears were copious during his funeral service and at the cemetery.

We always had a large garden plus milk cows and pigs so we had plenty of food even though I was born soon after the great depression. I had the impression that people in Fort Valley thought the Bassetts had plenty of money, but that was really not the case. Boble insisted on waiting until he could pay cash for our new home. Maybe this was because he was borrowing money each year to run the farm and didn't want any more debt. Later I remember any new furniture being bought for our new house was a big deal since money had been saved for some time prior to the purchase. As with many Southern farmers, we were land rich but cash poor.

Mama was a member of the Daughters of the American Revolution (DAR). I qualified to join both on the ancestry of Boble and Mama. Many years after I married and left home, I finally went to a DAR meeting and was so bored that I only attended one meeting, deciding that I simply couldn't sit through any more meetings with women obsessing about their various ancestors. The ladies were very nice to me and urged me to join, however, it reminded me of all the parties I had attended in Fort Valley to please my mother. Being from the "right" family was all important. I probably did not properly appreciate the prestige I enjoyed simply because I was a Bassett.

Chapter 3

Early Life on the Farm

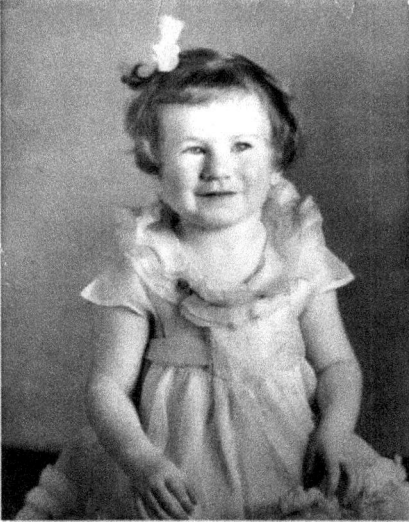

Evelyn at two years old, 1934.

SCHOOL DAYS
1938 - 39

Evelyn In first grade.

My father and his brother had inherited a thousand acres from their father. There were six large barns; one for the mules, one for the cows, two for storing cotton and two for storing wagons and other farm equipment. My cousin Patsy and I loved playing in the cotton which was stacked up almost to the ceiling of the barns. We would dig holes then tunnels connecting the holes together, an extremely dangerous activity since we would have been smothered quickly if some of the tunnels had collapsed.

Patsy, my cousin, who was only a few months older than I, roamed all over the farm unsupervised. We were expected to be back home by certain times, but the farm was our playground. We often walked to what we called the bird pond where Uncle Ralph and Boble would go bird hunting. To get to the bird pond, we had to walk through the "quarters" as the old slave quarters were called. These were four one room houses with an outhouse. The only heat was a fireplace and I assume some kind of stove although I don't recall ever going in any of the houses so am not sure about this. They had to walk about a quarter of a mile to get water from a pump and carry it home in buckets. There were four other houses on the place for the hands with similar setups for living, two several miles down the road in one direction and four houses off the main road in the other direction.

Uncle Ralph

Morris Dees, in his book *A Lawyer's Journey*, gave a detailed description of some of the houses of the Colored people living on his family's land. I imagine that our hands had a similar dismal situation in their small houses.

"The eleven people in Clarence's family lived in two rooms, sharing four iron-framed beds, mattresses stuffed with corn shucks. The boards for the shack had come from a run-down plantation home that had been demolished when Dee's family built a new house. The inside walls were covered by old magazine pages attached with flour paste. They were a feeble attempt to keep out the damp winter winds that snuck through the boards and roared through the open windows. You could see the tin roof above the uncovered pine ceiling beams. There was no running water or electricity. Oil lamps lit the drab interior. Heat was supplied by a single fireplace and a wood cook stove that sat in the corner of the small sloped kitchen at the rear."

There were many wooded areas still on the Bassett property. One was quite wild, having lots of weeds and brambles, but we children loved going to a little pond that must have been fed by some underground spring. This was the "wishing well" and we always took coins to throw in the pond. No one but Boble seemed to know where this magical pond was so we children never tried to go alone. We probably never would have found it since there was no path; it was also a scary place with all those trees, brambles and always the possibility of snakes.

I was in college when Uncle Ralph died from a massive heart attack. He was like a second father to me, really treating me like another daughter. Patsy and I often walked with him down to a road which connected to the Macon highway. We always called it the turn road. It was later renamed Bassett Rd. Uncle Ralph taught us some marches with cadences from his army days. "I had a good home and left, left, left. I knew it wasn't right, right, right". With Uncle Ralph's blessing Patsy and I tried chewing tobacco, but we found that disgusting so it was a one-time experience. What we really wanted to do was to smoke a cigarette; however, both Uncle Ralph and my parents were very opposed to cigarettes. Instead my uncle said we could smoke cigars; however we would have to smoke an entire cigar. We thought this was great but halfway through the cigars, we were getting sicker and sicker. We were in Uncle Ralph's bedroom where we often visited him. He sat across from us and kept insisting we had to finish those cigars which we reluctantly did but bolted out of the room to the bathroom to throw up as soon as we could. Neither Patsy nor I have ever had any desire to smoke cigarettes or cigars since then. That was a good lesson!

Dirt road connecting our road with the Macon Highway.

Living with an extended family was a great way to grow up. In order to give the cooks a day off on Thanksgiving and Christmas Day, both families went to the Perry Hotel. Perry was a nearby town where we went for various events. Each family would take a turn paying for the dinners – one paid for Thanksgiving and one paid for Christmas dinner. This was such a tradition that all of the many Bassetts from all over went to the Perry Hotel as part of a large family reunion in 2000. As far as I know the Hotel is still operating.

Another big event in Fort Valley was the annual Halloween Carnival held in the town square. Various organizations set up booths as fund raisers, but the big thing was the BARBECUE and Brunswick stew. A pig would have been roasting in a pit for days and my, how wonderful all of that tasted! I never went trick or treating; in fact I don't think I had ever heard of such a tradition until I moved to Maryland outside Washington D.C.

Another activity both families loved was our many picnics at Houston Lake. Back in those days you could swim in the lake or a pool and there were various picnic areas around with tables and fire pits. It was a real treat to take a ride in one of their commercial motorboats out across the lake. A favorite of the older children was a place with a jukebox where they could dance. Both families brought lots of food; hotdogs and hamburgers were cooked over the fire pits and we had a real feast. I particularly remember the fried chicken and egg salad sandwiches which were quickly devoured after a day of swimming. We were often allowed to bring one of our friends who lived on a dairy farm not far from our place. Becky remained a lifelong friend until she developed Alzheimer's about two years ago. The big event when we graduated from seventh grade was to go with our class to Houston Lake. Our tastes for fun were rather simple back in those days!

The old swimming pool in town had been closed when I was very young. The story I heard was it closed because some of the colored people had started going swimming after dark. I don't know if this was true or not. The pool was quite old and probably needed repairs anyway so that may have been the main factor.

Friend Mary Beck Johns, Marise, Patsy, brother Ralph and Evelyn.

The summers are extremely hot and humid in Georgia so children really wanted a place to go swimming. We loved Houston Lake but we only went there on special occasions such as holidays. Our main place to get relief from the heat was in Mossy Creek which is about two miles down the road from Pineola. There was a bridge across the creek where Boble would sometimes fish and catch perch; the colored people would fish for catfish which were big and quite dangerous if they cut you with their bony spines. We never went swimming near the bridge but went down a path that went further down the creek. It was actually more like wading because the water was not really deep enough to swim. The path was quite sandy and children often developed ringworm from walking barefoot in the sand.

One time several of we children were riding our bicycles down a steep hill above the creek. I kept urging my younger brother, Ralph, to go faster. He went so fast he went head first over the handle bars, banged his head and broke his wrist. He was in shock so I stayed with him as he lay down in the shade of a rundown old cabin beside the road. Patsy and my friend rode back home to notify my parents. After Boble took Ralph back home, our local doctor came out to set his wrist; I remember feeling really guilty hearing Ralph scream as he moved the bones around to put on a caste. Ralph tells me that he used some old newspapers to make a caste; while I don't remember that detail, Ralph over the years has often brought this whole episode up. I don't think he has ever forgiven me because he says I tried to kill him. Of course, he knows that is not true, but he does like to make me feel guilty!

Boble always had a number of mules, mostly to pull the wagons, but we children liked to ride the mules. They all had names which I don't recall; some were more stubborn than the others. We would ride them along Taylor's Mill Road which was often muddy after rains. We tried to steer the mules in the less muddy ruts, but they did what they wanted regardless of our urging. They also would stop often to eat the numerous blackberries along the side of the road. Apparently the thorns did not bother them. Obviously we had very little real control over our stubborn mules! On one memorable occasion, Ralph and I decided to hitch up one of the mules to a kind of buggy type cart that was supposed to just be used by our overseer. We went down our dirt road then turned onto the road that went to the Macon Highway. We were enjoying our escapade until right before we reached the highway. Our mule suddenly decided to veer off into the nearby woods. Nothing we could do would make our mule stop; it just kept on going, running into trees and demolishing our cart! Since we were doing this without permission, we both freaked out, knowing we were in big trouble. We finally decided one of us was going to have to go back home and report our dilemma. I think I was the one who stayed with our wayward mule while Ralph faced the music back home. We were not allowed to get near any mules for quite a while after that. I should add that we had one horse which was strictly for the overseer and when he used the buggy/cart it was driven by the horse, not a stubborn mule.

A vivid memory was all of the adults sitting on the front porch of the Bassett home with feet propped up on the banister telling ghost stories which abounded in that part of the country. I would start out the evening with them until Mama insisted I go to bed. Our part of the house was way around toward the back; it seemed like an eternity walking back there since the ghost stories really frightened me as a young child. My grandmother on Boble's side was into table tipping to communicate with spirits. One of the stories was about a disembodied voice speaking in Spanish although no one in her group around the table spoke Spanish. She passed over before I was born, but I could imagine her spirit still around. There were many ghost stories told while sitting on the front porch after dark. Three I particularly remember: a dog would suddenly appear alongside a carriage going down the road then quickly disappear after a short time; this happened repeatedly for over a year according to the tale. Another story was about footsteps heard in the attic of a house not far from us. This again happened repeatedly with no sign of footsteps in the attic dust. As with the dog, the footsteps would cease after a while but would begin again a few days later. There was never any explanation for this! However, the really scary one was about a ferocious animal suddenly appearing at the foot of the occupant's bed, snarling and terrifying the person in the bed. Then the animal disappeared! This supposedly happened at a house about two miles from our home. I believe the owner of the house moved out and eventually sold the house. As you can imagine, these tales really frightened me since I was only about five or six!

Patsy and I had a pet cemetery where we buried dead cats and birds we found around the farm. I think we even gave them names to put on their tombstones. We certainly never wore gloves so it is a wonder we didn't get contaminated with some kind of virus. Uncle Ralph fed the feral cats on the place once a week. He would get lots of meat scraps from the local market and call the cats. This was a weekly ritual in an open air shed and the cats seemed to know just when this would happen because literally dozens would show up. Cats would never be allowed in the house, but Uncle Ralph loved his cats. Between feedings they would forage all over the farm which kept the mice at bay so they served a good purpose.

During the hot summer Patsy and I played outside a great deal. We climbed trees and often went swimming in Uncle Ralph's fish pond. It had several different areas around a large rock in the center – quite artistic. We couldn't really swim since we were about seven or eight and too big for doing much swimming in such small areas, but it was great to cool off and apparently the fish didn't bother us. Uncle Ralph was unaware of this activity, but it was too hot for him to be outside. No doubt we would have been in big trouble if he had discovered our pool escapades amid his precious goldfish! Needless to say there was no air conditioning in those days, but the high ceilings of the house made it much cooler than the outside air so most of the adults stayed inside during the summer, leaving us children to do whatever we fancied.

Patsy and I loved climbing up into the rafter area of our barns. One of the barns housed the mules used to pull the wagons and the hogs that were butchered for food once a year; the hogs stayed mainly in the area outside the barn, a muddy mess most of the time. The whole area was, of course, fenced. I can't recall exactly how we were able to get up in the attic of that barn; however, I do remember the boar that would sometimes run after us so whatever we did had to be quick!

The cows were housed in another barn across the road adjacent to the acreage where Boble finally built our home in 1941. These animals were never killed for meat but kept for their milk. We always churned the left over sour milk for butter and buttermilk. The cow barn was another favorite place to play upstairs where the hay was stored. The obstacle there was a big bull that sometimes chased us all the way to the barn! We were really lucky to never be attacked; we were obviously adventuresome children!

One event on the farm that really bothered me was the annual clean out of the septic tank. There was a large round hole dug in the ground about six feet across. There must have been planks or some kind of cover because it did not smell most of the time. When it was cleaned, however, the smell permeated the entire property, front and back of the house. Apparently in those days there was no enclosed septic tank with a leach field as today. I can still sometimes imagine that smell; it was so seared in my memory.

The other event that really bothered me was the annual killing of the hogs. Their terrified squealing could be heard far and wide. I tried to get as far away from it as possible. I never witnessed how they were killed, but it certainly must not have been a humane act, however, I did enjoy our pork roast and the bacon that was cured in our smoke house. There were large slabs of meat hanging from a hook in the smoke house, so we had hams. I really don't know what method was used for the smoking process – one of those questions I should have asked. Boble loved pork brains which I think were cooked with scrambled eggs but I refused to ever touch them. After hog killing season Boble enjoyed liver pudding, another dish that I also never ate. There were no refrigerators with freezers in those days. In fact, we had only ice boxes for many years with a delivery of ice from the ice plant which eventually closed down with the advent of refrigerators run on electricity. There was a freezer locker plant in Fort Valley where we could rent a unit to store all of our roasts, etc. The town had electricity but none for many years in the surrounding rural areas such as our farm.

Patsy and I loved to play house. There was a huge fig tree in the back yard with branches that went all the way down to the ground. We would find several places for our rooms, using a broom to sweep the ground clean. There was lots of privacy because the foliage of the tree was so dense no one could see us from the house. Our other spot was the doll house which had been built before my birth for Uncle Ralph's older daughters. It was about seven by seven square feet with a small window and a door we could close so it was quite cozy. Actually my strongest memory of the doll house was the location for our various clubs. With some of the neighboring children we would form clubs, none of which lasted very long, but it was great fun using our creative minds to discuss various club businesses!

We lived in Peach County, so-named for the many peach orchards and packing plants in and around Fort Valley.

During peach season everyone would actually get tired of eating peaches, but we loved peach ice cream. We would gather on the long screened porch at the side of the house, all of us taking turns at churning the ice cream which was a labor intensive undertaking but well worth the effort. There is nothing better than homemade peach ice cream! Actually there is nothing better than a good Georgia peach. I would surely love to have one of those again.

The evenings were long during the summer months in Georgia. The children would play out in the front yard. One of our favorite games was "Simon Says". There was a long walkway then about eight steps leading up to the front porch. If you forgot to say "Simon Says" when given instructions on how many steps you could take, then you forfeit your turn. The goal was to see who could get to the top of the steps first. We would mark off hop scotch squares out in the dirt under the pine needles. Another favorite was crack the whip. All the children would hold hands then the leader would go as fast as she could, trying to have the last child fall down or at least no longer be able to hold the hand of the next child in line. There were many other games played outside after supper, all fun for us children except one game which holds very bad memories for me. See chapter on Sexual Abuse for an explanation.

Not so fun were the various children's diseases we all suffered. Measles hit me at an early age. Mine was a severe case making it necessary for me to be in the dark a lot since they were concerned about my eyes that are often affected by measles. I still think that my extreme near sightedness was probably the results of measles. Chicken pox followed measles with mumps waiting until I was a junior in high school. It was just understood that most children would have these diseases since there were no vaccinations at an early age as there are today. I was finally vaccinated for small pox when I was in the second grade. It left a sore on one's arm, leaving a scar which could still be seen many years later.

Then there was the nationwide polio epidemic. This meant that no children in Fort Valley were allowed in public places for fear of contracting this awful malady. We mainly stayed on the farm, but when my parents had to go into town and I went with them I always stayed in the car. I am not sure whether at that age I was aware of Franklin Roosevelt having polio; maybe I knew something about it because he would frequently go to Warm Springs, Georgia to swim in the mineral pool and receive physical therapy. This was no secret although supposedly many people did not know that he could not stand alone. His messages to the people were over the radio so this was not evident. Many years later when I was a teacher I was required to have an oral Salk vaccine for polio. I think this was a requirement to obtain a teaching position.

One of my good friends in elementary school was a victim of polio. From the time he was in the fourth grade George was in a wheelchair. We were always good friends, both playing clarinets side by side in our newly formed school band. He went on to become one of our honor graduates and I think I heard that he had a brief successful career but died at a fairly early age. Everyone liked George Hopkins, being very willing to give him a helping hand when we could. He was always cheerful despite his severe handicap. The only way to really understand the tragedy of polio is to have lived through an epidemic.

I was in the hospital twice at a very young age. There was no hospital in Fort Valley when I was young; later the town had Peach County Hospital but that was after I had moved away. We always had to go to Macon for anything serious enough for hospitalization. When I was about four years old, as we were driving home from town, I kept saying I had to go to the bathroom. There were few places in town to do this but the Gulf gas station at the edge of town did have a restroom. As my father pulled into the station, I opened the back door, fell out and apparently one of the tires rolled over my leg. I am not sure what happened after that except somehow I had a caste put on my leg. It may have been in the local doctor's office or the Macon Hospital. I just remember walking around the farm yard on crutches. The time I vividly remember being in the hospital was before I started school so I was quite young. All I know is I had a high fever of unknown (at least to me) origin. It was very scary being in a hospital alone at such a young age. I have the feeling the fever was so high I was hallucinating so obviously my parents were quite concerned. My impression is the hospital stay was about a week – a long time for a little child to be away from her parents. Since it is important to know one's health history, I should have asked my parents for more details but I obviously never thought to do that.

There was no Kindergarten and no eighth grade so I graduated from high school after completing the eleventh grade. This changed by the time my brother graduated; however, at the time I was very ready to leave high school. The only drawback was going to Agnes Scott College where almost everyone there had attended high schools with twelve grades and most were honor graduates. Although I was one of our honor graduates, there were only 26 people in our class so that was no big deal since there was very little competition. The students in my class were much more interested in football than any academic achievement! The Fort Valley football team won the Georgia State Championship for their class so every reunion I attended it was all about football; there was very little recognition for my having earned a PH.D. Ah well, that is the way it goes.

Chapter 4

World War II Recollections

Boble and Mama.

By 1941 when Pearl Harbor was bombed, my father had built a nice home across the road from the old family home. I remember hearing about it on the radio that Sunday. Soon afterward President Roosevelt announced that we were going to war. Everyone was shocked but there was no controversy since our country had been attacked. I was only nine but I remember that day clearly. Soon gas was rationed as well as sugar and other food items, but everyone supported the war and cooperated, not minding these inconveniences since it was a small sacrifice compared to the millions of young men who were being drafted and sent to war.

Our overseer at that time had only one son whom he and his wife adored. He was drafted into the army. We would get periodic reports on him since they were constantly worried that he might be killed. I would often go visit the Moxleys to find out if they had any more news about Earl. Fortunately he made it through the war, but he was a changed person when he finally returned home. He only stayed a short time before leaving his parent's home.

Downtown Fort Valley 1947.

Cochran Field was developed during World War II, a large Air Corp field located between Fort Valley and Macon, Georgia. Aunt Henriette began inviting young cadets from England who were training to be pilots to visit the Bassett homeplace. Four of the Bassett daughters, Marguerite, Beulah, Simone and Marise, were of a dating age so they loved entertaining the young men, mainly just walking around the yard and of course, there was always a good dinner or lunch. I was very envious of my older cousins. Finally my family also invited a British pilot to have dinner at our house. For some reason I decided to make some peanut butter cookies, one of my few culinary skills. However, I forgot to include one of the essential ingredients so the cookies turned out to be absolutely awful! I remember this because I had bragged about making the cookies to our English guest, Claude, and was terribly embarrassed that they tasted so terrible. During this time I became a pen pal via e-mail (not computer type but small letters on one page that were sent via airmail to communicate with the troops) with Claude's sister in England. That was an education about life in England during war time.

Fort Valley High School class of 1949. Evelyn 5th left, front row. George Hopkins in wheelchair.

I also sent many e-mail letters to my Uncle Roger who was serving as a chaplain in the South Pacific. I was very fond of

Uncle Rody (nickname for Roger) since he had taught Patsy and me how to swim when we were all visiting Grandmama and Grandpapa. He took us down to Indian Springs south of Atlanta where there was a large pool. He taught us to swim on our sides and to this day that is my preferred way of swimming. Unfortunately, swimming was a required course at Agnes Scott and when I was forced to switch over to overhand crawls, etc. I often felt I was going to drown. Diving was certainly not one of my skills either so I was relieved to at least pass the course!

Another memorable experience for Patsy and me was serving punch at the American Legion Hall in town. As I recall these were formal dances for all of the servicemen so we really dressed up for these occasions. Of course, we were too young for any of the young men to ask us to dance, but we really enjoyed watching all the dancing and girls with pretty dresses although we would have had a much better time if we could also have danced.

The day that peace was declared, my high school closed for the day. All the students walked to their respective churches to pray and give thanks for the war ending.

I am thankful to have lived during that war. It was so different from our subsequent wars, conflicts, etc. Everyone was patriotic and totally supported our servicemen. This had also been true during World War I. My father had been in the Navy during World War I and Uncle Ralph had been in the Marines. I heard some stories about the war, but Uncle Ralph who was wounded and gassed in France during that war never told Patsy and me any stories about his battlefield days. As with many veterans today, it was apparently a very painful memory in his life that he did not care to discuss. On the other hand, due to his background in agriculture, in the Navy Boble was assigned to duty as a pig inspector at one of the facilities furnishing food for the troops. That was a real sore point with my father since he had hoped to see some action overseas. As it was, Uncle Ralph was the war hero of the family and Boble had the full responsibility of taking over the farm for both families due to Uncle Ralph's various disabilities.

Uncle Ralph paid Boble rent each year for the use of his share of the land. That worked well until the death of Uncle Ralph then Boble had much difficulty trying to deal with Aunt Henriette who was always having some kind of disagreement about the rent and various other issues. Finally after Boble died, my brother Ralph was able to negotiate a division of the land which Aunt Henriette had previously refused to do. Of course, by then I had moved to California so was not privy to all the details.

Chapter 5

My Recollections of Colored People Living on the Farm

I had a nurse named Laura whom I adored. I know nothing about Laura's family or living conditions except that she lived on our place. One morning when I was about nine as I was getting dressed for school I asked my mother, "Where is Laura?" I don't know why I had a nurse at that age, but apparently I was quite spoiled and she even helped me get dressed for school many times. Anyway, Mama told me that she would not be coming back. I was told that she had gotten drunk and was in jail which now makes no sense. There must have been a lot more to the story than I was told. Perhaps she had been sent to prison for a much more serious offense than being drunk.

My father often received telephone calls from the sheriff late at night to come bail some of our hands out of jail for being drunk since Peach County was dry. Many of the Colored people would go into town on a wagon Saturday supposedly to shop but there may have been places they could get alcohol. At any rate, I was devastated to never see my beloved Laura again. I would surely like to know what happened to her. I guess another possibility is she was somehow killed and Mama didn't want to explain that to me.

Old Carrie was my baby sitter many times when Mama and Boble went out in the evening. She was cranky but she was always good to us children. I don't know if Carrie had a last name since all of the hands just went by first names. She was

37

always old in my eyes so her name was just Old Carrie. She lived in a long house with a small kitchen/sitting room on one end. It had a wood stove and there may have been a bed since there was no heat in the rest of the house. The very large room on the other end had a row of beds, and Bassett family ancestor portraits were all along both walls. I have no idea who if anyone ever slept in the beds but I do know that the portraits were hung there because Aunt Henriette refused to have them in the main house. One summer when I was at home from college, Carrie's house caught on fire. There was a bucket brigade with people drawing water from outdoor faucets but the fire was quickly totally out of control. At that time the fire department did not go to fires out in the country. I remember vividly watching this huge fire which no one could extinguish. It was seen as a lost cause early on so the little water they were able to transport went toward watering down the adjacent barn. So much for all the Bassett ancestor portraits! Aunt Henriette probably thought, "Good riddance", but it was a great loss for the rest of the family. Poor Carrie no longer had a home. She eventually moved into town to live with some friends. She was a grouchy old woman, but probably had rheumatism in addition to a very hard life so one could hardly blame her.

There was another fire on the Bassett farm. When I was about six years old and still living in the old homestead, Cousin Patsy and I were playing house in one of the very large closets filled with clothes. There were entrances to the two bedrooms on each side; Patsy and I had the stupid idea to light a candle since there was no light in the closet. In a short time the clothes caught on fire. I was terrified and ran to get under the bed. Patsy, more sensibly, told someone about the fire which resulted in another fire brigade which fortunately was able to extinguish the fire but not until everyone was totally freaked out, fearing that the whole house would go up in flames. To this day there are scorch marks in the closet which are shown to visitors wanting to know about life on a southern plantation. I was seldom punished, but this was one time the big switch came out. I felt really guilty so felt the punishment was justified!

One of the children's favorite people was Old Hiram. He lived in a tiny little cabin with an outhouse near the road. According to my brother, Ralph, Hiram supervised the women working in the fields, hoeing, etc. All I remember was Patsy and I visiting Hiram in his little cabin. We truly loved Hiram; he was so good to us. At Christmas both Hiram and Carrie would come up to our house and call "Christmas gift". I guess this was an old southern tradition dating back to the days of slavery. We always made it a point to buy a gift for both of them – usually socks or something practical. They had so little, they appreciated anything. Later I would hear that Hiram had moved into town and died by falling into a fireplace. He probably had a stroke. When I heard about this, I mourned, feeling I had lost a good friend.

Another Colored family I really liked was our Colored overseer and his wife. I would often sneak down to their house to eat dinner (we had supper in the South, not dinner; lunch was dinner). His wife Lilla May was a wonderful cook. She was a cook at our house for a number of years before they moved. However, somehow their food tasted better than what we had at home. Maybe that was because it was a forbidden escapade. Lilla May made a particularly delicious chocolate pie. I have never had any chocolate pie to match hers nor found any recipe for it. Once my parents found out I was eating at our Colored overseer's house on a regular basis, they sternly forbade me to ever visit them again. Later during my growing up we had two white overseers. I was friendly with them, but they were never as special in my mind as our Colored overseer.

Before leaving the subject of food, I need to say that Southern cooking is really delicious, mainly thanks to our good Colored cooks. Everything was cooked in lots of grease, fried food being frequently on the menu. We had lots of vegetables since we always had a garden, but really there was no regard for what we talk about as "healthy" food these days. My father died of colon cancer and his diet may have been a factor, but he certainly enjoyed eating before he became ill. However, we never used pesticides on anything we ate, just the cotton in the fields to kill the boll weevils. There was no such thing as GMO modified food and there was plenty of good fresh butter since we churned our own butter from sour milk. So maybe despite all the grease laden food, all in all the food was probably healthier than our food today.

My father's main crop was cotton. During cotton picking season Mama would drive into town early in the morning to pick up Colored workers to pick the cotton. She would make several trips because at times there were as many as 50 to 60 people picking cotton. This was long before there were any cotton picking machines. After my brother inherited the farm, he tells me that the Colored people were paid $2.50 to $ 3.50 a day, depending on how much they picked. During the time I was growing up they were probably paid much less. It was hot, back breaking work. One summer I asked my father if I could pick cotton and he agreed. I lasted about half a day. It was the most difficult work I have ever done in my life. I am in awe as to how these Colored people could last until almost the sun went down. Every day what they had picked was weighed and noted by my father who would then pay them at the end of the week. Ralph, my brother who had inherited the farm from Mama, says the tractor drivers earned $3.00 to $4.50 a day. The other main crops raised on the farm were wheat and oats. Even then there were combines and tractors that needed drivers. It was a better job than picking cotton, but it was still extremely hot. I don't know what any of them did about drinking water. One summer I sold soda pop from our refrigerator. What they really should have had was bottled water, but I don't recall any of them drinking water. They were in the fields all day so I presume they went to the bathroom in the fields. I felt for these people even then, but now all I can think is it was really like slave labor.

I want to again quote from Morris Dee's story about his childhood in Alabama:

> "Up until this point on the farm, everything was "men's work", but when the cotton plants pushed an inch above the earth, women (and often children) joined the men in the fields. With days lengthening, growing hotter, the hands labored with long-handled, eight-inch iron hoes from 6 A.M. to 6 P.M. (with one hour off for dinner, the midday meal) chopping nut grass, coffeeweed, and Johnson grass that threatened to choke the young plants.

> By the time the cotton was ready to be picked, the split bolls have become hard, thorny, unforgiving burrs which even the most talented fingers cannot escape. Experienced pickers pinched the bolls between their fingertips at its roots in the burr to bring it out cleanly in one pluck. But the action was repeated too many times to come away unscathed. If the burrs were the only thing to put up with, it would be bad enough. But there's the cramping of the hand, the sharp pain in the back from constantly bending over and dragging the cotton in the increasingly heavy sack slung over the

shoulder. And there is the unrelenting heat that the hands call the "bear."

As stated earlier, my short stay picking cotton was an eye opener as to the difficulty and what these poor hands were doing to earn a meager living.

Along this line of working on farms in the South, I want to include a long description written by my husband, Paul Mounts, a native of Kentucky. He writes about his experience as a young boy working in the tobacco fields. This deserves a separate chapter. Tobacco was not a crop grown much in Georgia. Unlike my early life, Paul was a true child of the depression. He is now 89 years old and a miracle of survival.

Chapter 6

Harvesting Tobacco

Kentucky tobacco field. James, Robert and Milton Mounts (Paul's dad).

My husband, Paul, had a very different childhood in Kentucky. While writing about the difficulties picking cotton in the South, I felt it important to include a first-hand experience of someone who was truly a child of the great depression and his servitude as a child working in the tobacco fields of one of his relatives. It left such a negative impression on his memory that Paul has included a discussion of his tobacco fields experience in his obituary which I asked that he write since I did not know Paul until he was 80 years old; therefore, my knowledge of his earlier life is somewhat sketchy.

43

A Boy Looks Back on the Farm

(Age nine to fourteen: 1939 - 1944)

In 1939 my mom, my older brother and I were still reeling from the Great Depression, trying to make ends meet after my dad left the family for 'greener pastures' without mortgage payments and three family members who did not rise to the level of his pleasure requirements. So, like many other kids who were abandoned by one parent – in this case a dad, my mother had to assume the responsibilities of two parents.

My Mom's first job as head of the household in the early 1930's was as secretary in a Jewelry store. I don't know what wages she earned in this job. Later she worked several years at a grocery store where she worked an average of 70 plus hours a week. Her $12 weekly salary was hardly adequate for the three of us to get by. Therefore, while mom worked at the store, my brother and I generated as much money as possible with odd jobs according to the season of the year. Other jobs Mom worked at brought in a little more money – Atlas Tack Company, and making bullets in a converted Chrysler Company factory for the war effort in the early 1940's. Both my brother and I were rewarded with a little better income from year to year as we gained experience and became more and more responsible.

Wages for my first year on the farm (1939, age 9) was room and board and one $25 payment directly to my mother at the end of the summer season when I returned home to attend school. During my stay with cousins I was given 15 to 25 cents each Saturday night when the family went into town to buy groceries and other supplies. Ten cents always went for 22 rifle bullets whenever they were available at the hardware stores, and the balance for ice cream and or candy. Every other Saturday night I was given an extra 10 cents for a haircut. (When I got a haircut it looked like a 10 cent job too!) On July 4th each year I was given an extra 15 to 25 cents to buy firecrackers at the Sebree Springs, the only public park that I know of in Webster County where families large and small came to eat watermelon and hot dogs while catching up on all the gossip going around. Wages for my second summer (age 10) was room and board and 25 cents a day, with the same amount of 'spending money' for items mentioned above. All those quarters were kept by my cousin and given to mom at the end of the summer.

The next summer (age 11) I was about to get into some 'real money' for my work – 50 cents a day plus a little 'spending money.' As noted above the money for working was always given directly to my mother to pay household expenses.

I don't remember what wages I received during the summer when I was 12 years old, but one can guess on the basis of prior and following years. But maybe that wasn't as important to me as the fact I was learning to smoke and chew tobacco, and even had opportunity to drink one or two beers and taste some genuine 'white lightning' brewed in a homemade backyard still in Sebree KY. This was in 1942 when WW II was going on. Most of our smoking material came in a 25 cent bag of crumbled tobacco, complete with bird feathers and whatever else just happened to get bagged.

I remember distinctly one day my cousin telling my mother about him looking across the pasture one day and saw puffs of smoke coming from the path over the rise. THAT, of

45

course, was me, smoking as I walked along the path between the two houses on the farm. I stayed with the owner's son and his wife; my brother got to stay in the big house. Mom was aghast that I would do such a thing, but didn't do other than scold me for my mischief.

Again, I don't remember the exact amount of money my cousins gave to my mother at the end of the work season when I was 13, because I never saw any of it anyway.

I do remember that my last summer of working on the farm was in 1944, age 14. I was paid $1 a day, BIG money, which went to Mom at the end of the season. During this season my uncle Ben promised me a new watch if I would quit smoking. I did, he didn't, without any reason for denying me the watch. However, quitting smoking was a reward in itself so I did not get further addicted to the stinking stuff.

When school was out for the summer or winter vacations, Claude Earl and I headed for work on the farm. One of the first jobs in late Spring or early Summer was to plant and cultivate large gardens of vegetables, including up to a half acre of beans (great northern, pinto, navy and butter beans, to name a few) and another quarter acre of potatoes.

Another major task was to help prepare seed beds for tobacco plants and later transplanting them into the fields. Tobacco was the primary source of income for many farm families in Western Kentucky. Even a small acreage allowance for tobacco was the most lucrative crop the farmers depended on for income for a whole year. Between working in gardens and tobacco fields we baled hay, planted and cultivated corn, wheat, oats, barley and soy beans; then ...back to the tobacco fields.

Tobacco plants required almost constant handling after pulling them from the plant beds and transplanting into prepared fields. The plants are very tender and fragile and must be handled like African violets, or similar plants. When the plants are eight to 12 inches tall they must be carefully examined for worms, twist off their heads, and of course, wipe the guts off on our pants. 'Worming' was augmented by occasional spraying of arsenic of lead or another more powerful insecticide dust. Only the mature adults were allowed to use the dust blowers, and they got to wear paper masks, as if that would help much in contact with such toxic chemicals. 'The help' had no masks or gloves, and had to handle the tobacco throughout the growing season in search of worms, coming in constant with spray residue on the leaves. Worms damage the quality of the tobacco leaf by eating holes in it.

Around this time in the growth process when the plants have grown to roughly 30 to 40 inches, the top is broken out so 16 to 20 leaves can grow wider and longer, and even lap between two rows. As growth continues, shoots (called suckers) emerge where the leaf adjoins the stalk. Those suckers must be broken out by hand as soon as possible to prevent more growth from pushing the maturing leaf off the stalk. Suckering is repeated as up to three new shoots appear, making it more difficult to break the new suckers over the stubs of old suckers. Ouch! I can still feel those stubs tearing into my young hands!

It is around this time that farmers invite neighboring tobacco farmers and their hands to help in this labor-intensive process. The farmer who owns the field agrees to help neighboring tobacco farmers in return with a similar amount of labor, or he may hire non-tobacco farmers and their families to help sucker his fields of tobacco. The fields in which I worked were large 'patches' (two to eight acres in a 'patch.' Therefore, my cousin (owner) had to hire available men or boys in the area to keep the work done on time. There were three black farmers in the area that would either bring or send their boys age six to 12 to work with us, and those boys must be able to keep up with the men or get yelled at.

Tobacco plants have a covering of sticky gum that adheres to hands and clothes like honey poured into and over a tight glove, and can only be washed off by a hard scrubbing with harsh soap and brushes. Hanging in the air above tobacco fields is a cloud of sickening sweet odor that makes a lot of workers sick. Since I was already somewhat sickly as a child, I had frequently had a difficult time staying at work to avoid being yelled at. But since I had to work, knowing that our family needed the money, I spent most days in the fields, regardless of how sick I felt.

Work days in the tobacco field started around 6 AM, after milking the cows in a dark stable, and a heavy breakfast. The only reason to stop work in the field was for a quick drink from a gallon jug with a gunny sack cover to keep it somewhat cool. The only reason to leave the patch before quitting for the day was to throw up, for 'nature calls' and to go for more jugs of water.

Dinner (lunch) was at 12 noon, and was usually consumed with hands and clothes thick with tobacco gum because it took too long to scrub them. There's a knack to eating bread with dirty hands, just hold a corner of a piece of bread by two fingers, and toss that dirty piece to the dogs. Back to the fields at 1 PM until 6 or 7 PM. When we quit for the day we scrubbed up and milked the cows before eating supper. By the time supper was finished we just about fell into bed for death-like sleep, hardly moving until someone shook us awake the next morning. Work in tobacco fields were LONG days, especially for a pre-teen!

When neighboring black men or boys came to work at 'our' farm, they did not sit at the table with the white folks to eat. They had to sit at a table on the porch or wait 'till the white folks had eaten. Even when we traded work with black farm neighbors, the same eating arrangements were observed - the white folks ate first in the black family's own house. I could NEVER understand that eating arrangement, and can't imagine to this day why they put up with it. I was told that 'blacks and whites just don't mix,' and that was that!

Harvest time is another ordeal in the tobacco patch. When mature leaves begin to 'ripen', on a hot sunny day, several workers launch into the task of cutting the stalks. The stalk is bent over with one hand while the other hand uses a 'spud' knife, an 8" to 10" steel rod with the blade crosswise on the end, to cut the stalk through with a quick jab. The cut stalk, about 36" to 45" tall and weighing 15 to 25 pounds, is then lifted up and carefully laid down in a swooping motion to avoid breaking the brittle leaves to be wilted by the hot sun. This process is no little feat for a 9 to 14-year-old boy, much shorter than a grown man!

After the leaves are wilted, each stalk is lifted high with one hand and speared with a spike onto a 5 1/2' long, hand split, oak 'stick'. Five or six stalks are speared onto one stick. Loaded sticks are lifted onto a 5' high flat-bed wagon and transported to the barn. In the barn, the 'sticks' are handed up one at a time to men standing one above another on 2"X6" tiers (rails), spaced approximately 48" apart to hold the sticks, allowing the stalks to hang freely while the tobacco 'cures' for up to three months. An average tobacco barn may have up to five tiers of sticks. I never worked up in the barn because I was too short to straddle the gap between the tiers and lift the heavy sticks while balancing to keep from falling.

In late Fall or early Winter, when the leaves are dried sufficiently, and yet damp enough to prevent crumbling or tearing when handled, the sticks are handed down from the tiers to workers at a table. The leaves are then stripped one at a time from the stalks and sorted into piles according to their quality and tied into 'hands' of 10 to 15 leaves; the hands are then placed on a basket-type pallet. The quality sorts are 'leaf', used primarily for cigars and cigarettes; 'lugs', for lesser quality smoking and chewing tobacco; 'trash', for still lesser quality smoking and chewing; and lastly, 'sheep wash', used for snuff, pesticides, and other products for its high nicotine content. 'Sheep wash' is rightly named for leaf and stem pieces that fall from the tiers and 'washed' by sheep housed in the barn to get the full effect of killing fleas and other parasites by toxic nicotine. Of course, bird feathers, poop and whatever else tend to stick to the cured tobacco. Wow, doesn't that sound tasty???

When enough pallets of tobacco are ready for sale, they are transported to a warehouse in the bigger city for auction. The pallets are arranged on the floor with paths between just wide enough to allow the auctioneer, sellers and buyers, e.g. R J Reynolds and others, and the farmers involved to walk through, examine the quality of each pallet and make offers by auction. Since many tobacco farmers chew the stuff while the auction proceeds, and need to spit, some actually spit onto the pallets of tobacco. Of course, they won't spit on the path where they must walk!

Tobacco, through all its processing is never washed. That much moisture would cause the tobacco to mold or rot, destroying the product. The only cleaning process I know about throughout the cycle of raising tobacco is ultraviolet light applied somewhere along the processing line. Can you imagine tobacco user's lack of hesitation in putting that stuff into their mouths??? Yuck!

Shortly after I turned 15, I had an emergency appendectomy, and after getting out of hospital I recuperated, quit school, and got a job at a store in downtown Henderson that sold glass, paint and wall paper. I had to quit school to hold the job, but learned skills that are still important to me today. And, by the way, I made $15 per week, and got to drive the company's 1946 Chevy pickup making deliveries.

After this work experience I was reenrolled in high school. I worked several months in a grocery store, helping in the meat department while making 15 cents per hour. BIGGER money, right?

For more of Paul's story, read *Cosmic Relationships* which tells more about Paul as an adult, his past lives and his relationship with Evelyn.

Chapter 7

Fort Valley State College

On November 6, 1895 an interracial group of fifteen Black men, many of them former slaves, and three white men petitioned the Superior Court of Houston County, Georgia to legalize the creation of a school "to promote the cause of mental and manual education in the state of Georgia"; the Fort Valley High and Industrial School was born. The group's leader, John Wesley Davison, himself a slave as a child, was hired as its first principal. My great grandfather, Stephen Elisha Bassett was one of the white founders.

The students built many of the original buildings on campus. Much of the funding came from its neighbors, uneducated African Americans who sacrificed their own meager money to make possible the education of others. In addition to educating people to be teachers, it produced other professionals. One of the first graduates of the young school was Austin Thomas Walden, who graduated in 1902 and became the first black judge since Reconstruction. In 1932 the state of Georgia acquired the school and designated it a four-year college named Fort Valley State College. A number of other majors were added over the years and the college has produced many outstanding leaders for the Black communities in this country.

In 1972 Georgia segregation practices were under full-scale assault, and 29 white parents filed a lawsuit to help integrate Fort Valley State College. By that time there were white students living in the town and surrounding areas who wished to attend a local college. The lawsuit was successful and there are now white professors as well as many white students. In 1996 the institution obtained university status.

When I was growing up the college seemed to be a world unto its self, located in the Colored part of town across the railroad tracks. I had been aware of the part my great grandfather Stephen Elisha Bassett had played in the founding of the college. When I went back for a very large family reunion in 2000, part of the Bassett history tour was a visit to the university. Even then I was very ignorant as to the very interesting story about the college. I am including a brief version of the history I learned from Wikipedia, but I would encourage my readers to do their own research since the college is a bridge into the modern world from the time of slavery. I am sure it played a large part in preventing lynching and other terrible treatment of Colored people in other states and parts of Georgia. The founders of the college felt that education was the key to becoming productive citizens which is so true. Perhaps the college is also the reason Fort Valley escaped the riots in other parts of the South. I was no longer in Georgia during the civil rights marches, etc., but Mama would have told me about it had this happened. This does not mean there did not continue to be much prejudice against the Colored people in Fort Valley, but many of them, by then, had acquired businesses and built very nice homes. However, the movie theater had closed since the whites did not want an integrated theater. The city pool had closed many years ago. There was much resistance to integrating schools, but that did eventually happen. I discovered that there was never a Ku Klux Klan in Fort Valley which was, I theorize, mainly due to the founding of the college which produced many educated Colored people.

It was very noble of Stephen Elisha to help found an educational institution for the Colored people to attend, but from everything I have heard about my Great Grandfather, he totally ruled his family with everyone being rather afraid of him. He was a minister, but did not like the local Methodist church, so he built his own church, a Congregational Church which stood throughout my childhood until it was finally torn down to build a new library on the site. The land was donated by my father for the new structure.

Chapter 8

Segregation in Fort Valley

Fort Valley High School band.

The entire time I was going to school in Fort Valley, the schools were segregated. The old grammar school (we did not use the term elementary) was a two story building. The auditorium and some of the classrooms were upstairs. It was a real fire trap, but we were fortunate enough to never have any fires while I was there. There was no cafeteria so we brought lunches which we ate out on the playground unless it was raining. We never heard of kindergarten so first grade was when I began my education. One fond memory was soup day. One day of the month we would have soup and peanut butter sandwiches in the classroom. This may have just been a custom in my first grade since I don't recall that happening in any of my other grades. My eyesight was terrible so I could not see the letters of the alphabet posted around the room. Somehow I learned to read, but I didn't even know I couldn't see well until the fifth grade when our eyes were tested. Another memory was standing to sing with other students in a room off of the stage of the auditorium which was upstairs. It was May and really hot. At least in the upstairs classrooms windows could be opened but this room had no windows that I recall. At any rate, midway through our singing, I fainted, totally passing out. The teacher was obviously quite alarmed so called my parents to come take me home.

Grades one through five occupied the old grammar school building. Grades sixth and seventh were in one wing of the high school. Grades eight, nine, ten and eleven were high school. It seemed that many of the small towns in Georgia had only eleven grades which turned out to be a real disadvantage when, as stated earlier, I went to college and had to compete with the top graduates from large city high schools. One of my best friends at Agnes Scott College was from Tifton, Georgia. She also had only completed eleven grades and both she and I really struggled our freshman year even though we were both honor graduates in our small towns. Fortunately I finally learned to study and had a B average by the time I graduated. I realized that I probably did very little studying while in high school. My father was on the Board of Education which may have been a factor in my good grades. I recall receiving an A in history from a teacher who reportedly never graded nor returned any tests. How this teacher kept her teaching position is a mystery except she was from one of the "good" families in town and everyone liked her. This was the teacher who was in charge of the study hall where I was trying to take the entrance test for Agnes Scott College. She kept a running conversation with the boys in the class about their basketball games, making it very difficult for me to concentrate on a very important test. Years later I found graduate school very easy so was then grateful for the strong academic training I received at Agnes Scott.

My freshman year my high school finally had a band. Mama wanted me to play a cornet but the band only needed clarinet players. Later when my brother was old enough to join the band, he played a cornet. We played at all the football games, even going on a bus to a few out of town games. I played solo clarinet so thought I was a rather accomplished clarinetist. When later at an Honors Band Camp held at Milledgeville State College with band students from all over the state, I quickly learned that I was totally lost when assigned a second clarinet part. Still, I naively thought I would be fine joining the Agnes Scott wind ensemble my freshman year, but that did not last long. If I couldn't play the lead tune, I just faked knowing what I was doing; however, this was very stressful and I am sure I did not fool the teacher. Our first high school band director was young, good looking and had an amazing talent for shaping students who knew nothing about musical instruments into a fairly decent band. He was later replaced by a very different but equally good band director whom I later ran into when I was attending Sacramento State College for graduate work. I always loved Dr. Corder who by then was teaching at a college further south in the California central valley. We had a delightful lunch together before he left to return home. By that time I was working toward being a school counselor, my clarinet days far behind.

During all of my school years there were schools for Colored people on the other side of town. I really know nothing about them except I would presume that the teachers were mainly graduates of Fort Valley State College. I understood that the Colored high school had outstanding football and basketball teams. My high school football team won the Georgia State championship one year, but they probably would have lost any games they had played against the Colored teams. Of course, due to segregation that never happened.

In our history class we read about the War Between the States; it was never called the Civil War. Every year on the fourth Monday in April there was a school assembly commemorating our heroes in the War Between the States. This was usually a program put on by the United Daughters of the Confederacy (UDC). This was always our Southern Memorial Day. It was not until much later that I found out that Memorial Day in the rest of the country was in May.

When I was living on the farm none of the Colored people went to school. Living three miles out of town plus going to the schools on the other side of town was not an option for any of our farm families. Most of them could not even read. They were still slaves in a sense because they were totally dependent on my father. They paid no rent; when they needed to go to a doctor my father took them and paid the bill. As mentioned earlier, if they went to jail he went into town, paid a fine; then they were released and returned to the farm. Actually it was a co-dependent relationship since Boble was dependent on them to run the farm. Before much of the modern farm machinery was invented, there was a tremendous amount of manual labor required.

One of the women who had lived on our place took care of Mama after she had developed breast cancer. Frances was a child when they lived in the country, but her family finally moved to town. After my father died, Mama moved into town and gave our house to my brother Ralph who then took over the farm. Rain or shine Frances would walk from her house which was in the Colored part of town to Mama's house and later all the way to the nursing home on the Macon Highway where Mama finally had to be moved. I was grateful for all she had done for my mother so I made it a point to send her a Christmas card with a small check every year even after Mama died. After a long delay, she would finally write back a long articulate letter with a beautiful card. It finally dawned on me that it was her daughter who wrote the letters. I always sent Frances a Christmas letter talking about my life that year, but her letters never reflected this. She probably was not able to read them. Her daughter had joined the service and Frances was always very proud of her. One year I never heard back from my Christmas card/letter so I assumed that Frances had died. She was a brave, caring soul, a true Christian.

Although segregation was no longer legal, there was plenty of prejudice among the white people in Fort Valley. This didn't extend just to Blacks but to Jews. There was one Jewish family in town who owned a clothing store. We never shopped there I assume because they were Jewish. Mama and Boble thought that my Aunt Henriette was really Jewish. Maybe that was one reason they didn't like her. One of the stories I heard about the Bassett family was about one of Boble's brothers who was involved with a Colored woman. Apparently he really cared about her, but as the result of this relationship his family had nothing more to do with him. This was a "hush, hush" story so I never heard any real details as no one wanted to talk about it.

Chapter 9

Am I Prejudiced?

I always liked and felt sorry for the Colored people, but after I inherited some property in town from my mother, I must say that somewhat began to change my feelings. I sold a store that was turned into a beauty shop by agreeing to let a Black man buy it with very little down. At one point he fell behind in his payments. He sent me a letter pleading to give him more time to come up with back payments. He had made a lot of improvements to his business and I really liked the man so I let it go until he could finally pay off the entire loan which he eventually did. You couldn't ask for a nicer man. He had made many improvements to the property which I appreciated.

Another store was bought for very little by a man who had a business making tee shirts with logos. There was paint all over the floor when I came back to Georgia from California one time to check on things. The store was an absolute disaster. I finally sold it to him for almost nothing just to unload it. This man was no one you would want to know.

Then I had the problem of what to do with the large 100 plus year old house in town where Mama had lived after Boble died. It had marble fireplaces, good draperies and was lovely during my mother's life. I was not able to sell it so found a realtor who handled rental property. There was an excellent renter for about five years but then they found another location and moved. My original realtor no longer wanted to handle the property so I found another woman whom I thought was a legitimate realtor. She rented it to a Black woman who had an extended family. She was in no position to rent the house to begin with because part of the rent came from the Social Security payments from her parents who died after a few years. She then decided she absolutely must buy the house because "God told her to buy it". My so-called realtor, a white woman, was a friend of this woman and did no real credit checks so she convinced me to let the woman buy the house with a very low down payment and I would carry the loan. Part of our sales agreement was her replacement of the roof which by that time was in very poor condition. I foolishly agreed to her buying the house. Within a short time she stopped making payments on her loan to me, lying every time about when she would pay and make the repairs included in our agreement. She eventually declared bankruptcy. The bankruptcy court said she would make low payments over a long period of time on the loan. The roof had never been replaced nor even repaired. It was actually falling in toward the back of the house. The buyer had stopped making any payments on the bankruptcy agreement so I hired an attorney, a Black woman, to see what could be done. The attorney never did anything, not even answering my letters. It turned out that she was the wife of the Fort Valley city attorney who wanted to buy the property. After hiring another attorney and getting the title back in my name, he gave me a ridiculously low offer on the house which I turned down. Not long after, the City Attorney declared the house as a public nuisance that needed to be torn down. When the woman finally moved out, my new attorney offered to clean the house out, and there were three dump loads of debris in the house. It apparently was a swamp of trash. Although I couldn't prove it, I suspect there was a lot of drug dealing and using going on in the house. Finally, I just wanted to unload it so deeded it to the City of Fort Valley. They sold it to the same City Attorney who had originally made a low offer on the house, the husband of the Black attorney who would not answer my letters. He has used it for his office complex and made improvements on the property. The whole situation smelled of a very shady deal but at least I no longer had to be concerned about any property in Fort Valley. All of this property had been inherited from my mother and since I lived in California at the time, it was very difficult to handle rental property from that distance. This experience left a very sour note regarding some of the so-called Christian Black people in Fort Valley. The woman who gave me all of the grief about this last property was a big member of her church. According to my so-called realtor, she had a beautiful voice and the people in her church loved her! She made it sound as if having a beautiful voice qualified to buy a house. This makes one really question Christians who seem to be completely unethical. I don't know anything about the spiritual beliefs of the city attorney and his wife, but they certainly didn't value honesty. It was a huge relief to finally no longer have any concerns about any Georgia property even though I lost quite a bit just to unload it.

I have never thought I was prejudiced. However, as I have grown older, I have to face the fact that the people in my family were prejudiced and that probably rubbed off on me at a subconscious level. When my father died, there was a service at the local Presbyterian Church. Quite a large number of the Colored people from our farm attended, but they had to stand up at the back of the church through a very long service. I don't know if someone directed them to do this or it was just they did not think they would be welcomed if they tried to sit down in the pews. I believe it was the latter. I think Boble tried to do the right thing by his hands and I honestly thought that they loved Boble or Mr. Noble as they called him. I was sitting at the front of the church, totally bereft because I adored my father. I have no memory of any of the Colored people going to the cemetery after the church service, but I was sobbing so much, I was only vaguely aware of anything happening at the grave site. I really don't know how the Colored people on our place felt about my family. They always addressed me as Miss Evelyn, Mama as Miss Edith and Boble as Mr. Noble. I never remember them being rude in any way, but what they discussed when away from the family I will never know. I have talked to my brother who inherited our farm as to why he thought Boble did not do anything to improve the living conditions of the Colored people on our place. He explained that every year Boble had to borrow money from the Farm Loan Company in order to farm for the next year. If there was a good crop, he repaid it and had some left over, but if the weather was unseasonably bad, he would have difficulty paying the loan so he always had to keep a certain amount liquid to be able to repay the loan in bad years. This was an uncertain way to live, but apparently that is the way most small farmers operate. Growing up I was sheltered from any of our financial problems; however, my brother, Ralph, had to face the situation head on when Mama deeded the farm to him after Boble died. Ralph does tell me that he had running water piped to some of the Colored houses but that was the extent of any renovations to the Colored houses. By that time many of the families had moved into town, but Ralph still had to hire drivers for the tractors and other farm equipment.

Chapter 10

More about Prejudice

After graduating from college in 1953, I taught school for six years, first in Georgia, then in Maryland. Despite the fact that the Supreme Court had ordered schools integrated in 1954, I never had a Black student in my class. This was even true when I moved to California in 1958. It was not until I was a counselor at a Title I school in California, that there was a Black student in any of the schools where I taught or was a counselor. I remember one student well because he was an angry little boy, considered a bully on the playground. I started a counseling group of students whom I suspected were being abused at home. This boy was one of those students. Since he was only in the third grade at the time, I felt that confronting his parents would only make matters worse. Instead I had him in my office for counseling and he seemed to gradually become less angry. However, within a year his family moved away. He is one of my students whom I have often wondered what became of him as an adult. There was another Black student who was extremely smart but also getting into many fights. He lived with his grandmother who was very concerned about him, knowing that his parents had been very abusive. His hero was Magic Johnson since this boy was an outstanding basketball player and his ambition was to be a professional basketball player. I lost track of him when he went into the seventh grade. I always hoped he would achieve his goal.

Many years later when I had completed my book, *From Sirius to Earth,* I was looking for someone to proofread and maybe do some editing on the book.

One of my clients was a very attractive Black woman who was a librarian at the University of Davis. She agreed to look at my book but didn't get far before she returned it and told me I needed to take some classes in writing. Now I have never pretended to be a great writer since I think of myself as a therapist and not an author, but she was not even nice about the situation. I had another woman edit the book and she made very few changes, complimenting me on my writing. Anyway, fortunately that did not totally discourage me since I have written three more books since then. However, I did give a lot of thought as to why this woman reacted the way she did. I concluded that maybe she objected to my saying in my book that the Colored people on our place loved my father. This was originally included in the brief summary of my life; however, it was deleted in the final version since it may have been offensive to others. The notion of cruel masters of southern plantations was no doubt true in many cases, but my father was never cruel. After World War II he wrote *A Constitution of the United Nations of the World,* a testament to his love of humanity and the world. However, I really have no idea how the Colored people on our place felt about my father. Did they love him? I now rather doubt it.

Later, I had a Black client who had graduated from medical school and was very successful in his profession. His interest in past life regression therapy was to understand why he was so different from the other members of his family. He came from a large family; four of his brothers were in prison and one was a drug addict. My client was married to a beautiful white woman and he felt there was a great deal of prejudice toward him and his wife because of the marriage. He described his wife as a caring, gifted woman in her own right and despite the feelings of others against them, it was a happy marriage. As usual we spent the entire first session just talking. At some point I may have said I grew up in Georgia. I remember commenting, "Wouldn't it be nice if Blacks all believed in reincarnation?" Since a number of my white clients had recalled under hypnosis that they were Black slaves in the Old South, my thinking was we experience lives in many different races and countries. Each lifetime is temporary, giving the soul many different experiences. For various reasons souls choose to incarnate to have a new experience and hopefully to evolve to a higher level. However, since the therapy session was about my client and not me expressing my beliefs, I didn't elaborate on my remark. At any rate, he did not come back for another appointment so I am assuming he was perhaps offended by my statement about Blacks and reincarnation. My Georgia background may have been seeping through our session because I felt rather uncomfortable, not knowing what terminology I should use. For some reason I felt intimidated; this was the first in-depth conversation I had ever had with a good looking, well-educated Black man. I thought "Blacks" was the most desired designation at that time, but possibly he wanted to be called African American. Whatever, I had hoped to clarify some points when I saw him again, but that never happened.

Chapter 11

Sexual Abuse as a Child

At the time, I did not think of my experience as sexual abuse. It was only after watching the confirmation of Bret Kavanaugh for the Supreme Court and the tearful testimony of Christine Blasey Ford that I once again visited that painful time of my life. Like Christine, I cannot give exact details because I am really not sure of my age when this happened. I am guessing about nine or ten.

The four episodes of sex abuse are still crystal clear in my mind to this day. As mentioned earlier, some neighbor children, several of my cousins and I often played games in the yard of the Bassett home. There was a spotlight anchored in one of the pine trees out in the yard so our games often went on after dark during the hot summer months. One of the neighbor children was four years older than I. My parents had never discussed sex with me so I was totally naïve in that department, therefore, I never said no to the neighbor boy's sexual advances so I felt it was my fault. Toward the end of one summer Mama asked me if this boy had ever tried to put his hand up my skirt. I denied this, being too embarrassed to tell her what really happened. Apparently he had tried this with my cousin Patsy and she told her mother who then told my mother.

The first time sexual abuse occurred was when the neighbor boy and I were hiding out in the chicken yard. For the game "give me a wave" (much like hide and seek) we usually had a partner since often this was after dark. While there seemed to be what would be called intercourse, there was apparently no penetration because I don't remember any pain or bleeding. I think at the time I was just curious since I had been taught nothing about sex matters. The next time this happened was on a grassy strip down by the mule barn. Subsequently, there was just fondling, once in the hay loft over the barn and then in a small tool shed by the barn. I believe by then I was starting to protest, but he was four years older than I and quite persuasive. He was a teenager and I was still only a child; I feel sure he must have been aware that what he was doing was wrong. This was almost 80 years ago, but the memory is still seared in my mind. Christine Blasey Ford gave credence to the imprint in the brain from sexual trauma; however, the male congressional bullies totally negated this.

Fortunately when Patsy told her mother about this boy, his coming down to our house was stopped. Both my father and mother were the ones cutting the ties with the neighbor child which was certainly fortunate. I never told my parents about what had happened to me because I had the definite impression that anything sexual was really bad. I felt guilty and at fault for what happened to me since I never definitively said NO.

Since we lived three miles out in the country, the school bus picked us up every morning. It really bothered me that he and his sister were on the same bus. I remember eating almost no breakfast because if I did, I felt like throwing up. This went on almost daily unless I could persuade Mama to drive me to school. The strange thing was at the time I never connected the abuse with my nausea. It struck me during the Christine Blasey Ford hearing that she often had claustrophobia due to her feeling of being smothered by Kavanaugh. As I grew up and started to date some, I would often throw up prior to the date or even during the date. One very embarrassing time was when four of us were attending a military ball in Macon for ROTC cadets and their dates. I remember walking on the street after we had a light dinner of hamburgers and throwing up all over the sidewalk. My date was very kind but I was humiliated. Another time when I was home from college for the summer, a very eligible man who had been an All American football player at Georgia Tech, asked me to go to dinner at the Perry Hotel. I ordered what appeared to be a delicious (and expensive) dinner but felt so nauseous that I could not eat anything. That was the last time he ever asked me for a date which really disappointed my parents. I still did not connect my nausea with the sexual abuse.

The same thing happened when I was in college and was invited to fraternity parties at Emory University and Georgia Tech. I often simply would not go because I was afraid I would throw up. After graduation when I met my first husband, he invited me to dinner and I remember thinking this might be a serious relationship because for the first time I thoroughly enjoyed the dinner and had no feelings of nausea. So hopefully that dismal chapter of my life had been resolved.

However, that is not the end of the story. This same boy married one of my high school classmates so they were at all of the high school reunions I attended. I always totally avoided him as much as possible, but as I was leaving the first reunion I had attended at a classmate's home, he approached me and offered to take me home. I was staying at a friend's house nearby, so declined. There was no way I was going to get in the car with him. I continued to avoid him as much as possible at subsequent reunions I attended.

In the meantime I heard that my abuser had gone to federal prison for some kind of fraud. I don't remember the details but I thought that was karma working. Much later after he was released, he started visiting my mother who at that point was living in the town of Fort Valley since my brother Ralph had inherited the farm after Boble died. When I went home to visit Mama one summer, this arrogant man made it a point to come over and visit, acting as if nothing had ever happened. I thought he had a lot of nerve but regretfully I never confronted him; possibly he had other victims out there who did confront him. When you hear about the MeToo Movement, it seems that there are many women who were abused but never reported it until much later when more of the abuse problem was out in the open.

In looking back on this whole abuse episode, I am amazed at the power of the subconscious mind. It would have been helpful if I could have figured out why being with boys equaled being nauseous, but I simply never connected the two. There was no physical reason for my many episodes of throwing up. It was similar to having anorexia except I did not force myself to throw up - it just happened. I was very slim but had no problem with body image so trying to lose weight was not an issue. Including this story in my book was not an easy decision but perhaps it can be helpful to other girls who have had similar situations. Therapy during my teen years might have been helpful but that never occurred to my parents as far as I know, although I am sure they were concerned over my condition.

Chapter 12

Prejudice and Evolution

I was in Japan counseling students at an Air Force Dependent High School during the time of the civil rights marches. Our only news from the U.S. was in the Stars and Stripes military newspaper that was basically a propaganda paper for the military. It did not discuss what was going on in Alabama, Martin Luther King or any of the other "bad" news in our country. Even when I returned to California, somehow the news in the South did not seem to be affecting us very much. However, once a Southerner, always a Southerner. I would never have moved from the South except I married a Georgia Tech engineer who was hired out of college by the National Security Agency (NSA). This required a move to the Washington D.C. area. I continued to make regular yearly trips back to see my parents until 1980 when Mama died. After that I seldom went back to Fort Valley except to inspect various properties I had inherited and to attend a few college reunions. Even now when I meet someone from the South there is an immediate bonding with a kindred soul.

Just growing up in the culture of the South, however, seems to give a different ingrained prospective on racial issues from most of the people in the rest of the country. A personal example of this was when I dated a psychologist in California after the death of my husband, Wally Fuqua. I was not really attracted to him, but he was extremely intelligent and we had many intellectual discussions. I remember his asking me, "What is your opinion of the cause of the Civil War. Was it slavery or states' rights?" Without a great deal of thought, I replied, " States' Rights." My guess is that would be the answer still of most Southerners. In a round about way that may be true since it was about the right to own slaves, but if asked that question today, I would answer "Slavery".

In examining my feelings about prejudice, I have to say that I consciously am not prejudiced. Knowing what a very difficult life the Colored people on our place experienced has given me an extra empathy I believe for any Black people I have met since moving away from Georgia. I am appalled over much of what I read about the Southern states these days, and I would have been delighted if Georgia had elected a Black woman as governor. What a remarkable day that would have been!

In considering my various relationships with African Americans over my long lifetime, my conclusion is they are in various stages of evolution the same as people in every race. I have no doubt that Old Hiram was a much evolved soul. It would be interesting to know why his soul chose such a difficult lifetime. It may have been to balance some karma from another lifetime or just an experience his soul needed to learn certain lessons. In the case of my client who was a doctor, he too was probably quite evolved but his brothers were much younger souls, maybe doing the best they could, considering their lack of Earth experiences. Going to prison they would hopefully learn some important lessons and be able to have a better lifetime in the future. As to the other Blacks on our farm, they were in various stages of evolution. Patsy and I never had any fear of the Colored people on our farm even though we wandered quite far at times away from our homes. This is my philosophical viewpoint now after learning much about the evolution of the soul. However, this understanding does not negate my deep feeling for the difficult life of the Colored people on our farm. It also gives me great empathy for the struggle many of these people are experiencing today.

people as we think. It also gives us great confidence, for it

Chapter 13

Concluding Thoughts

Earth is an interesting experiment, having people of so many diverse races and various stages of evolution. One of the roles of the more evolved souls is to assist our brothers and sisters of all races to be able to raise their vibrations and therefore, become more evolved in their consciousness. I am aware that I was born in an African tribal community; had a number of lifetimes in the Orient; many lives in Egypt; one in Spain, one in Medieval Europe, a number of lifetimes in South America; some in Ancient Greece; as well as many others of which I am unaware. It is said that the food one prefers and the places one would particularly like to travel are indications of where one lived in past lives. I have been fortunate enough to travel to Egypt, Greece, and Peru, places that especially attract me. I kept hoping for some Déjà vu experience where I would just KNOW I had been in that locality. However, the closest I came to this was at Machu Picchu in Peru when I left the rest of my traveling group to climb to the top and spend time in the Lookout Tower. As I sat there on one of the ledges of the windows looking out over the rest of the mountain meditating, I had an overpoweringly peaceful feeling. It was as if I never wanted to leave that spot. I received no details of what this meant, but I certainly felt as if I had been there before.

I hope that in my work as a counselor and teacher to many students and counseling clients over the past sixty years, my main job in this lifetime has been accomplished. I have always tried to assist all of them to become more evolved souls.

Appendix

Pineola

The Bassett Homeplace has always been known as Pineola, a name derived from all of the tall pine trees in the spacious front yard. After my father died, as stated, my brother who inherited the farm was finally able to reason with Aunt Henriette and the farm was divided between the two families. Each of Uncle Ralph's daughters inherited a section of the land which they later sold; Aunt Henriette stayed in the homestead house until due to her ill health, she moved to Indiana to live with her daughter Simone; my cousin Patsy finally inherited the house and lived there for quite some time when her children were young.

Patsy eventually sold the house and an Englishman bought it, making huge innovations in order to modernize it. This included installing central heating and air conditioning; however, as I understand it he seldom stayed in the house and it was finally again on the market for sale. The current owners, Delise and Paul Knight have continued making many improvements on the house and yard. They have a website, *Pineola.com*, which gives a long history of the house and Bassett family. In May 2000 they hosted a large Bassett family reunion. My late husband, Col. Edwin Cook and I attended and I met members of the various branches of the Bassett family whom I had never met. There is a long description of this reunion on their website.

A few years later the Knights had a barn my father had built moved from its location down the road to their backyard where it was completely renovated. They advertised it for weddings and other events as "The Barn". While I totally appreciate all of the work they have poured into my old homestead, I am at a loss to understand how there is very little ever mentioned about my family who lived in that house for eleven years before Boble built our home across the road. There is much to do about Aunt Henriette being a war bride and Uncle Ralph being a war hero. In the meantime Boble was the brother who ran the farm and worked from sunup to sundown during the growing season, making it possible for Uncle Ralph's family to live in the old homestead and entertain all those English cadets. However, I strongly believe that my father was a much evolved soul who dearly loved Uncle Ralph as not only a brother but his best friend. Although he hated farming, he never seemed to resent Uncle Ralph. The problem for both Boble and Mama was Aunt Henriette who always seemed to resent both of them.

Paul and Delise Knight are both lovely people and I assume they just don't know the real story about the two Bassett families! Of course, this is because they were learning the history mainly from Simone who was the main motivator connecting the place with the Bassett history. Aunt Henriette lived in Indiana with Simone many years before she died, so there was a strong bond between her and her mother.

If I were into fiction writing, an interesting novel could be written based on various family relationships! This book just touches on some of the underground conflicts among the various actors in our family. As in most families, the past is often romanticized and that is the image that Delise and Paul wish to project. Considering all the work they have done to make the old homestead indeed a place of beauty, they deserve to make their own story about their home. I still have very fond memories of Pineola and greatly appreciated the Knights hosting Bassett reunions which took a tremendous amount of work and organizing.

I want to end this book quoting a tribute to Pineola written by my cousin Patsy's late husband, Russell Hilliard: He gifted us with these beautiful words at the year 2000 Bassett reunion.

Sign erected by Delise and Paul Knight.

Pineola, I love you for the Bassetts who first gave life to you and renewed it from generation to generation: for Stephen Elisha who framed you in his heart and formed you in the field from tall Georgia pines. Pineola, I love you for your hall so wide and long, with your inner depths for memories and your outer doors for welcomes. Pineola, I love you for your ceilings, built high for coolness in your antebellum summers, but well lighted with crystal chandeliers to call all eyes upward in recent years. Pineola, I love you for your closets, both the high and the low, seasoned with your scent of cedar and your mysteries of voices from ages ago. Pineola, I love you for your porches that, breathing honeysuckle's sweetness, not only opened out to your birds, your flowers, your peaches, and your pines, but also to the lovely neighbors of Fort Valley and to the larger community of the world. Pineola, I love you for your children, among America's sturdy stock. You protected them to play in the softness of your cotton and to grow with your fields of grain.

I was indeed blessed to grow up in such a home!

Grandmama, baby Evelyn, Mama and Great Grandmother - 1932

Barn before remodeling.

Barn after remodeling.

Tom Thumb wedding. Evelyn on the left and Patsy on the right - about age 8.

Uncle Roger. Chaplain, South Pacific, World War II

Uncle Ralph and Aunt Henriette.

Uncle Ralph, Aunt Henriette, five daughters and Evelyn.

Mama and Boble.

Thank you for reading this book. Your comments would be welcomed either on Amazon or via e-mail (emfuqua@mycomspan.com). Be sure you give the title of Fuqua Book or it may go into spam if you use my e-mail.

You may be interested in my previous books, all available on Amazon or www.emfuqua.com.

From Sirius to Earth: A Therapist Discovers a Soul Exchange

Cosmic Relationships: Exploring the Soul's Journey from Off-Earth, Earth Lives, and Reincarnation

The Wisdom of Athor: Messages from a Member of the Council of Twelve on the Etheric Plane of the Star System Sirius

You Are Wonderful: Improving Children's Reading and Self Esteem

www.ingramcontent.com/pod-product-compliance
Lightning Source LLC
Chambersburg PA
CBHW060121050426
42448CB00010B/1978